GET REAL
FOR MAJOR SCALE DUETS

by Wynn-Anne Rossi and
Victoria McArthur

Patterns for Success

There are three possible ways to play the scale duets (student primo part) in this book.

1. Many students and teachers will choose the *two-octave (parallel motion) version*, which is notated throughout the book in every key.

2. If you are just beginning your study of major scales, you and your teacher may choose the *one-octave version*. This is not written out throughout the book, so you will need to memorize the pattern so you can play it in the keys which you will learn. This is not difficult if you notice how many times you will play the scale. A sample is included on this page in the key of C.

ONE-OCTAVE VERSION

To be played either hands separately or hands together, in any key.
Notice that the student part (primo) starts on measure 3 of the teacher part (secondo).

3. The most challenging version is the *two-octave (contrary motion) version*. It is identical to the two-octave (parallel motion) version written throughout the book, except for measures 13 – 16, which are different. Below is a sample in the key of C.

TWO-OCTAVE VERSION (CONTRARY MOTION)

To be played either hands separately or hands together, in any key.
Notice that the student part (primo) starts on measure 3 of the teacher part (secondo).

FJH1188

Twinkle, Twinkle Little C

Secondo

W. Rossi

Twinkle, Twinkle Little C

Primo

Ragtime G

Secondo

W. Rossi

Ragtime G

Primo

With charm (♩ = ca. 120)

Both hands 15ᵐᵃ (two octaves higher)

"D" Caribbean

Secondo

W. Rossi

"D" Caribbean

Primo

All-American A

Secondo

W. Rossi

All-American A

Primo

Beautiful E

Secondo

W. Rossi

Beautiful E

Primo

Honey B Swing

Secondo

W. Rossi

Honey B Swing

Primo

F Impressions

Secondo

W. Rossi

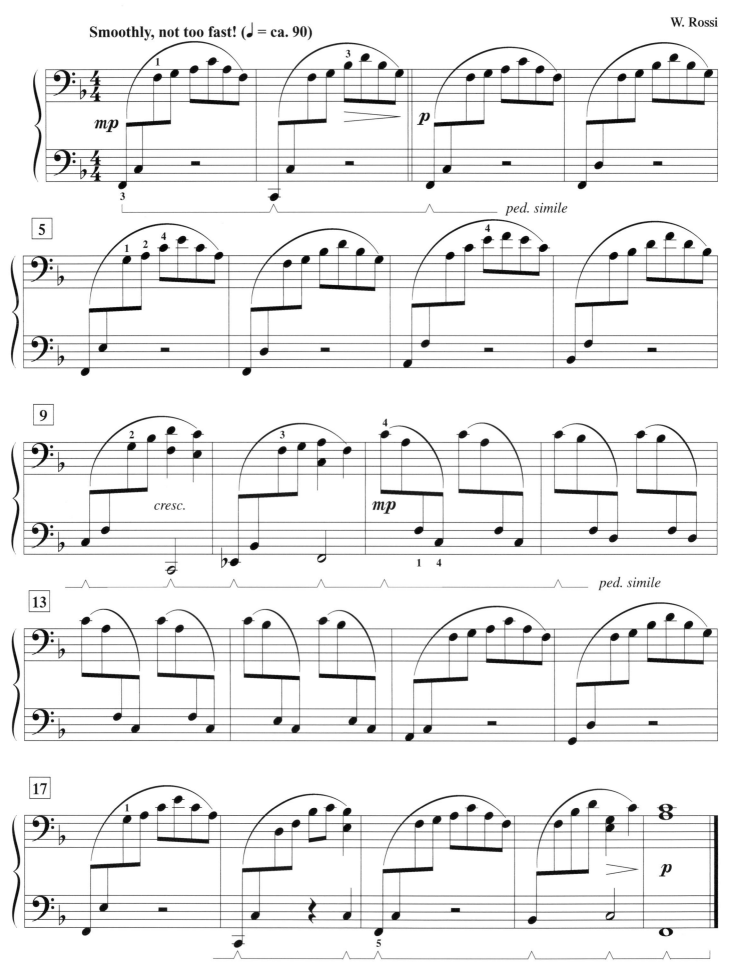

F Impressions

Primo

B♭ Boogie

Secondo

W. Rossi

B♭ Boogie

Primo

FJH1188

E♭ Exercise

Secondo

W. Rossi

E♭ Exercise

Primo

Adagio in A♭

Secondo

W. Rossi

Adagio in A♭

Primo

Tango in Db

Secondo

W. Rossi

Tango in D♭

Primo

G♭ March

Secondo

W. Rossi

G♭ March

Primo

Scale Facts

Scales are built from patterns of whole and half steps.

**A half step is the smallest distance on the keyboard—
from one key to the very next key.**

Sometimes half steps move from a white key to a black key:

A black key to a white key:

Or a white key to a white key:

A whole step is made up of two half steps.

Whole Step and Half Step Pattern for Major Scales:

All major scales are built from a pattern of whole steps and half steps.
This pattern is what our ears recognize as sounding major.

W W H W W W H

Study the example of the E major scale to see how the pattern above looks in an actual scale.

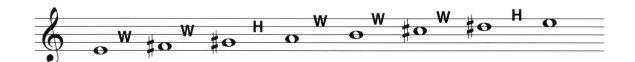

To figure out how to play a major scale starting on any key, simply play the first key as you say "start." Then move to the next note a whole step higher, and so on through the pattern. You usually will need to play some black keys as you proceed through the pattern. (C major is the only exception.)

Feeling Sharp In A Major Way!

There is an easy way to figure out the number and names of the sharps in each scale.
Study the chart below as you learn each sharp major scale.

Major Key Name	Number of Sharps	Names of Sharps
C	0 sharps	None
G	1 sharp	F♯
D	2 sharps	F♯, C♯
A	3 sharps	F♯, C♯, G♯
E	4 sharps	F♯, C♯, G♯, D♯
B	5 sharps	F♯, C♯, G♯, D♯, A♯
F♯	6 sharps	F♯, C♯, G♯, D♯, A♯, E♯
C♯	7 sharps	F♯, C♯, G♯, D♯, A♯, E♯, B♯

Notice that each sharp major scale name (C, G, D, A, E, B, F♯, C♯) is the interval of a 5th apart.
Starting with the key of C (0 sharps), **move up to the 5th note** of that scale which is G (1 sharp, F♯).
Then, move up to the 5th note of the G scale, which is D, and so on. Sometimes this pattern of
moving by 5ths is called the Circle of Fifths.

Have you noticed that the names of the sharps themselves are also a 5th apart?
If you start with F♯ (ALWAYS the first sharp in any key), go up a 5th to C♯, then to G♯, and so on.

Major Flat-tery!

The flat scales, like the sharp scales, follow an easy pattern.
Can you figure out the pattern on your own after looking at the chart below?

Major Key Name	Number of Flats	Names of Flats
C	0 flats	None
F	1 flat	B♭
B♭	2 flats	B♭, E♭
E♭	3 flats	B♭, E♭, A♭
A♭	4 flats	B♭, E♭, A♭, D♭
D♭	5 flats	B♭, E♭, A♭, D♭, G♭
G♭	6 flats	B♭, E♭, A♭, D♭, G♭, C♭
C♭	7 flats	B♭, E♭, A♭, D♭, G♭, C♭, F♭

Notice that the flat scales are also a 5th apart, but this time you **move down by 5ths** (easy to
remember since flat means to "move down"). Starting with the key of C (0 flats), move down a
5th to F (1 flat, B♭). Then move down a 5th for B♭ (2 flats, B♭ and E♭), and so on.

Notice that the names of the flats themselves are also 5ths apart. The first flat in any scale is B♭.
Move down a 5th to find the next flat (E♭), then A♭, and so on.

The Scale Detective

Now let's see how well you understand what you've read as you solve the mystery of
the missing notes for each of the scales below. Notice that you will need to use each letter in
the music alphabet only once when spelling the notes of a scale. Award yourself **2 points** if you
get the correct answer all by yourself. Award yourself **1 point** if you get the correct answer,
but have to look it up. (The answers are listed at the bottom of the page.)

Points (1 or 2)

1. The **second** note of the A major scale is ___.   _____
2. The **second** note of the E major scale is ___.   _____
3. Starting on B♭, the next note in the major scale is ___.   _____
4. The notes in the B major scale are B, C♯, ___, E, F♯, ___, ___, B.   _____
5. The notes in the G♭ major scale are G♭, ___, ___, C♭, D♭, E♭, ___, G♭.   _____
6. The **flats** in the scale of D♭ major are B♭, ___, ___, D♭, ___.   _____
7. The **flats** in the scale of A♭ major are ___, E♭, A♭, ___.   _____
8. The **sharps** in the scale of F♯ are ___, ___, ___, D♯, A♯, ___.   _____
9. The **third** note in the B♭ major scale is ___.   _____
10. The **third** note in the E♭ major scale is ___.   _____

More Mysteries To Solve

1. All major scales follow the pattern of W, ___, H, W, W, ___, ___.   _____
2. The scale of E major has ___ sharps.   _____
3. The scale of ___ major has 3 sharps.   _____
4. The scale of C♯ major has ___ sharps.   _____
5. The scale of ___ major has 2 sharps.   _____
6. The scale of ___ major has 3 flats.   _____
7. The G♭ major scale has ___ flats.   _____
8. The scale of F major has 1 flat, ___ (*name the flat*).   _____
9. The scale of ___ major has 2 flats.   _____
10. The A♭ major scale has ___ flats.   _____

Your Total Mystery Points Are: _____

Answers:

The Scale Detective Answers:
1. B
2. F♯
3. C
4. D♯, G♯, A♯
5. A♭, B♭, F
6. E♭, A♭, G♭
7. B♭, D♭
8. F♯, C♯, G♯, E♯
9. D
10. G

More Mysteries to Solve Answers:
1. W, W, H
2. 4
3. A
4. 7
5. D
6. E♭
7. 6
8. B♭
9. B♭
10. 4

FJH1188

Hearing Major Scales

Your teacher will play one mistake in each major scale below.
Circle the note where you hear a mistake.
Hint: You may wish to point to each note as your teacher plays.

Teacher: Play one incorrect note for each scale.

Major Scale Reference Chart*

C MAJOR

G MAJOR

D MAJOR

A MAJOR

E MAJOR

* Scales are presented in the order of the Circle of Fifths.

B MAJOR

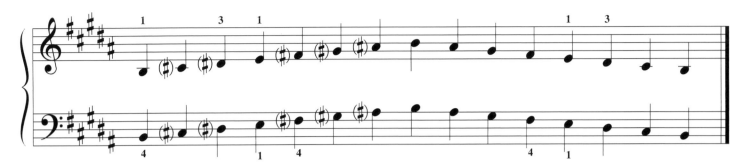

C♭ MAJOR

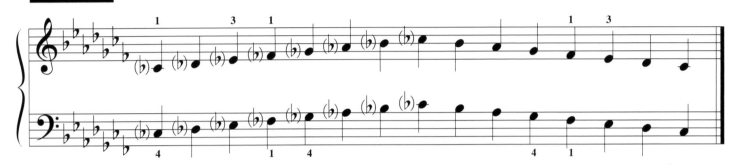

F♯ MAJOR

G♭ MAJOR

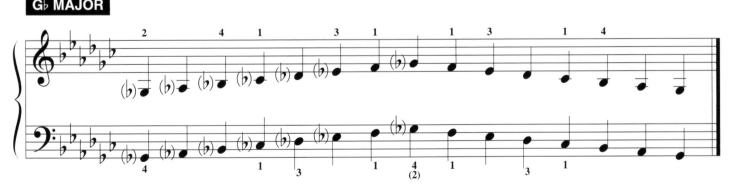

C♯ MAJOR

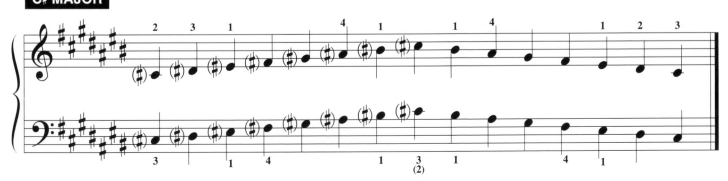

34

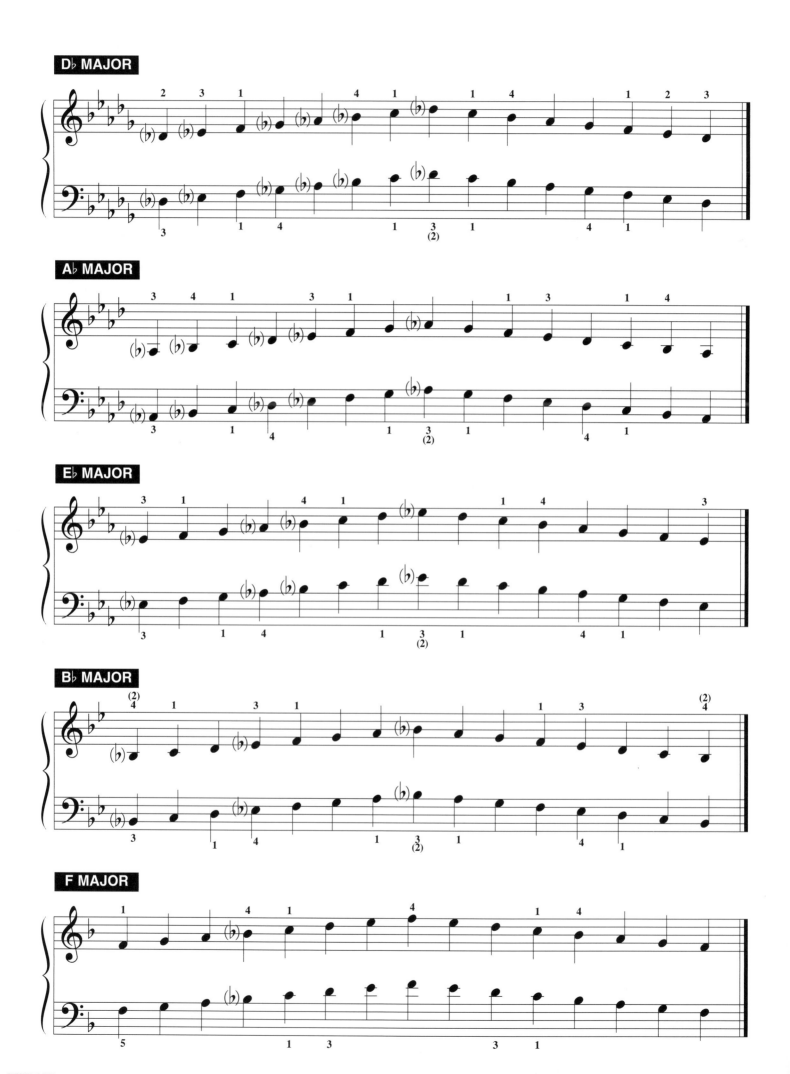

Fingering It All Out

Scale fingering is easy to learn with accurate practice.
That means that you need to use the **same** fingering
every time you play each scale.

Here are some basic fingering rules:

- The fourth finger usually plays only once in each major scale.
  Memorize where finger 4 goes.

- Thumbs land on the tonic note (scale name) in white key scales.

- If there is a B♭ in any scale, the right hand will play it with finger 4.

Fingering Groups

Certain scales "group together" according to their fingering. This makes them easier to learn.

- C, G, D, A, E, and B major scales all use this fingering in the right hand: 123 12345

- C, G, D, A, E, and F major scales all use this fingering in the left hand: 54321 321

- B major begins on finger 4 in the left hand; F major finishes on finger 4 in the right hand.
  (B **B**egins and F **F**inishes on 4.)

- B♭, E♭, A♭, and D♭ major scales all use this fingering in the left hand: 321 4321 3

Putting a Finger On It!

Fill in the blanks below.

1. The **right-hand** fingering for G major is: __ __ __ __ __ __ __ __.

2. The **left-hand** fingering for E major is: __ __ __ __ __ __ __ __.

3. The **right-hand** fingering for E♭ major uses finger __ on B♭.

4. The **left-hand** fingering for A♭ major is: __ __ __ __ __ __ __ __.

5. The **right-hand** fingering for F major is: __ __ __ __ __ __ __ __ (see p. 34).

6. The **left-hand** fingering for B major is: __ __ __ __ __ __ __ __ (see p. 33).

Scale Workouts*

These workouts are to be used each day before your scale practice. Just like sports,
scale-playing is athletic and involves many active movements of the fingers, hands, and arms.
Because of this, you need to get in the good habit of warming up before playing. Good luck!

Repeat each workout, playing faster each time. Listen for evenness.

WORKOUT 1 (R.H.)

WORKOUT 2 (L.H.)

*Although the workouts are best suited to the keys of C, G, D, A, and E major, other scales may be used.
(When using other keys, alter the fingering to fit the scale.)

WORKOUT 3 (R.H.)

WORKOUT 4 (L.H.)

Review Game

FLYING HIGH AROUND THE PLANET OF 5ths!
A journey through the sharp and flat zones.

Directions: Beginning at Middle C, take a shuttle journey to the keys your teacher chooses. Play the scale for that key. Continue on through as many sharp or flat zones (keys) as your teacher selects.

Note to Teacher: You may either choose keys in order (C, G, D, etc., or C, F, B♭, etc.), or you may select keys in random order (e.g., C, E♭, A, etc.).

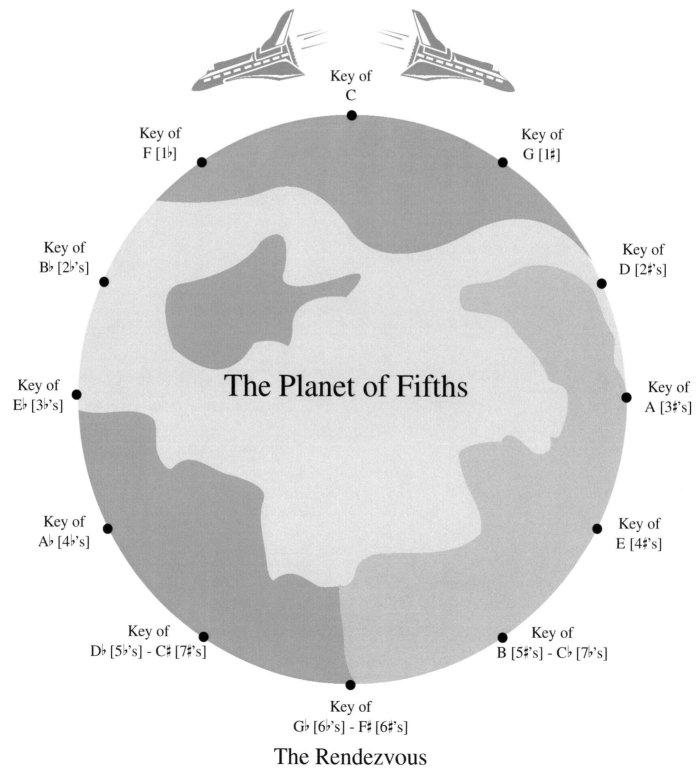

Key of
C

Key of
F [1♭]

Key of
G [1♯]

Key of
B♭ [2♭'s]

Key of
D [2♯'s]

Key of
E♭ [3♭'s]

The Planet of Fifths

Key of
A [3♯'s]

Key of
A♭ [4♭'s]

Key of
E [4♯'s]

Key of
D♭ [5♭'s] - C♯ [7♯'s]

Key of
B [5♯'s] - C♭ [7♭'s]

Key of
G♭ [6♭'s] - F♯ [6♯'s]

The Rendezvous

Scale Practice Flashcards
(to add variety to practice)

I'M FEELING FLASHY TODAY!

Student Directions:
Cut out the flashcards following the dotted lines, then shuffle them. Draw one from the stack, and follow the practice directions with the scale(s) you have been assigned, or other scales of your choice.

CUT HERE

Play *staccato* and *forte (f)*.	Play *legato* and *mezzo piano (mp)*.	Play *staccato* and *piano (p)*.
Play your right hand *forte (f)*, and your left hand *piano (p)*.	Play your right hand *piano (p)*, and your left hand *forte (f)*.	Play your right hand *legato*, and your left hand *staccato*.
Play your right hand *staccato*, and your left hand *legato*.	*Crescendo* when going up, *diminuendo* when going down.	Choose your own dynamic.
Make your scale sound: exciting, sad, angry, peaceful (choose one)	(fill in your choice)	(teacher's choice)

FJH1188

40

CUT HERE

Play *staccato* **and** *piano (p)*.	**Play** *legato* **and** *mezzo piano (mp)*.	**Play** *staccato* **and** *forte (f)*.
Play your right hand *legato*, **and your left hand** *staccato*.	**Play your right hand** *piano (p)*, **and your left hand** *forte (f)*.	**Play your right hand** *forte (f)*, **and your left hand** *piano (p)*.
Choose your own dynamic.	*Crescendo* **when going up,** *diminuendo* **when going down.**	**Play your right hand** *staccato*, **and your left hand** *legato*.
(teacher's choice)	**(fill in your choice)**	**Make your scale sound: exciting, sad, angry, peaceful (choose one)**